GEORGE SAITOH

LI'L HAT & HOLD STILL

GEORGE SAITOH

LI'L HAT & HOLD STILL

2 one-act plays

Janus Creations

2017

CONTENTS

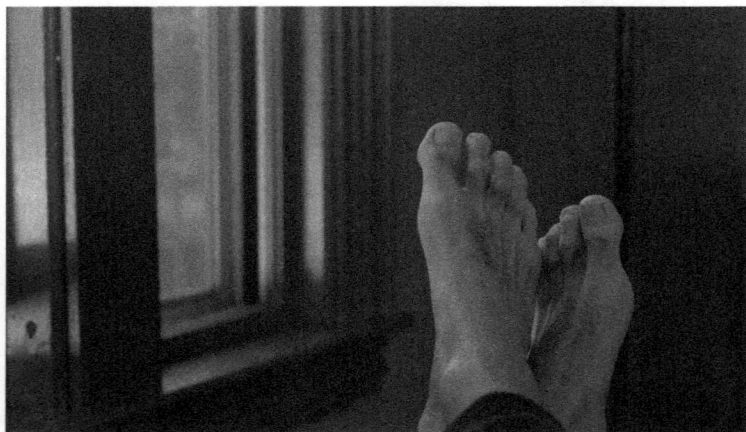

To Maho

LI'L HAT

CHARACTERS

Man

Woman

Teenaged boy

BLIND

When I'm blind I'll see
the wind battering blackthorns,
morning milk warming away pins and needles
from sitting too long, arms wrapped around knees
in the alcoves of empty days
& nights splinted to a pipebomb
loaded with people,
stones from a cornfield
& sloes,
each one pricked for the gin.

Scene: Man and woman in the kitchen of a modest house. The walls are half painted with a roller. The man is standing with his back to the audience. His knuckles are pressing down on the countertop for support. His head hangs heavy. Beside his hand on the countertop is a bottle of crimson nail varnish.

Standing behind him, the woman looks around the room. She looks all over him from his feet to his head, and down to his hands on the countertop, and the nail varnish. Approaches him a little too quickly she checks herself, as if to get it right.

His shoulders heave and he sighs. His wine-colored sweater is baggy from being worn and put back into the closet too many times without washing it. It looks like somebody else's sweater.

Sensing shame she moves in closer. Very slowly and gently she inserts a hand under his sweater and begins to stroke his back up to his neck. With her other hand she touches his knuckles on the countertop. She strokes with both hands, repeatedly, while observing his reactions with a patient smile on her face. He doesn't move. He releases another breath, same as before.

MAN   Didn't you see him?

        At these words she moves closer until her body contacts his. She steps onto her tippy toes and cranes over to kiss his neck. This is less a kiss—a gift—than it is an exploration, an invasion. Her lips move lightly and drily around like a fly, and her eyes rove emptily as her mind processes and considers.

Didn't you fucking see him?

WOMAN   I saw him, love.

She goes on stroking and kissing. He remains rigid. He releases a long breath. We are unsure if it's not, at least partially, a gasp of pleasure.

Did it upset you?

She goes on kissing and caressing as she waits for his reply. The longer it goes on the more we feel a mechanical, relentless and irritating quality. As it goes on, she—and audience—starts to become aware of how she is dressed, how she holds herself. She sniffs, her nose is a little congested. She sniffs again, then goes on kissing, with more seriousness. She re-enforces her smile. She is wearing navy slacks that hide the contours of her legs and hips. He shoes are functional, rather ugly and large and we can see white socks. Her hair is trimmed tight to her neck and thick and bouncy on top. Her head is very feminine and fragile but some jerkiness combined with her staring quality makes it birdlike. Her neck seems exposed, looks vulnerable to being wrung, and once that idea has entered into thought it remains there and her neck becomes a focal point, irreconcilable with the sturdiness of her feet.

MAN   Did it upset me?

WOMAN   Yes, love. Did it?

A teenaged boy enters and takes up a position on the fringe. He is wearing a baseball cap, black jeans, black t-shirt and basketball trainers. He has a small trick bicycle with nut extensions on the back wheel for standing on. He begins to perform complicated turns. Sometimes he falters, or falls. Then he tries again, unfazed and utterly absorbed.

MAN   Did his face upset me?

WOMAN   Yes, love. Did it?

He shakes his head slowly and under tight control—it is hard to know what is being negated: her question or something else, perhaps everything. She continues her caressing and kissing.

The boy continues his bicycle tricks. After a while she speaks again, kissing between phrases.

You know, love... I was thinking a moment ago...I was thinking back to when I was expecting...

His body stiffens some more. She waits a moment, registering his reaction before continuing.

I remember imagining the face...what it would look like.

We cannot see the boy's face, it is covered by the shadow of the baseball cap's peak.

I used to wear that li'l hat...the li'l French hat

with the black rabbit fur…when I was seven
months…because it was January.

*She gives a slow chuckle that sounds sarcastic.
She smiles as if realizing, though only we can see
her face. She goes on kissing his neck.*

MAN   You imagined.

*She pants suddenly and her movements take on a
flush of urgency.*

WOMAN   Yes, love. And those black boots I used to have.
The ones you said you could hear coming a mile
away.

*She chuckles again. His head sags slightly. He
releases a long breath.*

MAN   It seems like only yesterday. Doesn't it?

The boy makes a flourish on the bicycle.

WOMAN   Remember you used to wear your shoes
without socks?

*She stops kissing and moves slightly back and
stands squarely on her feet. She looks him up and
down, from head to feet. She chuckles and it
sounds like a sneer.*

"I've enough gadgets on me," you used to say.
Remember?

*She maintains the gap and gradually stops
moving her hands but keeps them in position,
ready to start up again. This withdrawal has a
visible effect on him where its application
appeared to have a lesser one. She doesn't speak*

now, just stands there, waiting. Her face still has an expression of false certainty but now she seems willing to alter course to move things forward to the goal. He seems to be trembling, and she does not seem to be unsatisfied with that reaction.

She sniffs to clear her nose. The sound is quite a bit louder than before. It is a sharp hiss that sends and involuntary shiver down his spine. She records this and re-applies her hands as if to soothe him. She leans in and gives him another kiss on the neck. Then she steps back again and stills her hands and waits.

The boy continues his act on the bicycle.

The man begins to tremble again. He reaches a hand up and it shakes as he goes to open the cupboard door. She responds by following his hand with her own and covering his, keeping the cupboard door closed.

Did it upset you?

His hand drops back down onto the countertop, and hers with it. She begins to caress him slowly again with both hands. This time his body gives a great heave. He releases a long, quivering breath. She leans in closer and begins to kiss him on the neck again.

It took a lot of guts.

He turns his head a fraction and hesitates before speaking.

MAN   What did?

She caresses him with greater urgency at his response.

WOMAN   This, love. Remember the first time?

His body stiffens. She strokes more. He suddenly relaxes and his head slumps. She slows her caressing right down and kisses him on the neck. He has a defeated air about him now. To her this seems to be progress. He slumps a little more and knocks the nail varnish bottle over. He releases a sigh.

Don't worry, love. It's only my nail varnish.

He raises a hand to the cupboard door, more feebly than before, and tries to open it. Once again she raises her own hand, more quickly than the last time, and stops him. Their hands remain raised against the door for a moment, then slowly return to the countertop. He stiffens, turns his head slightly to look at the varnish bottle, then picks it up and holds it in his fist. She chuckles once again at which he seems to tremble.

MAN   Gripe water.

WOMAN   No, love. It's only my nail varnish.

He slumps and releases a loud breath.

What about the gripe water?

MAN   I never use the word "gadgets".

WOMAN   Gripe water is for colic, love. Go on.

His body heaves and he seems to be in great pain,

which, if declared, could cause him to disintegrate. She chuckles again.

Tell me about the gripe water, Mursheen.

Each time she says 'gripe water' he winces.

Gripe water. Sure that's what they use for colic.

He shakes his head with great control of the movement.

Gripe water, love. I know what it is. It's what your mother would have given you when you were a li'l baby.

He begins to tremble violently and his legs buckle.

It's just for the colic. That's all gripe water is.

His trembling subsides and he stiffens again.

Sure that's all.

MAN   That's all?

WOMAN Yes, love. That's all. For to ease a touch of colic. That's all.

MAN   That's all.

WOMAN That's all it is.

She makes an urgent claim on his body by moving up against him, caressing with new care and kissing his neck and laying her hand against his back. He holds steady and clenches the nail varnish bottle more tightly.

Come on.

She steps back a fraction and pats him on the knuckles and on the back, gently, beneath the sweater.

Come on, love. Let's go upstairs.

He raises the hand halfway to the cupboard, from under her patting hand, and then hesitates. She watches, ready to stop it when it reaches the cupboard door but it doesn't. It comes back down to the counter of its own accord. He straightens up and takes a deep breath. His shoulders heave, his arms drop to his side and he clenches his fist.

Come on.

He doesn't move, apart from his head, which tilts back, as if trying to remember something.

Come on, Mursheen.

He seems to wince. Then he places his hands back on the counter and slumps his head between the shoulder blades. She thinks of something while rubbing his back. With her other hand she dithers—removing it from his and then replacing it.

It's ok. We can stay here for a while.

MAN   Here.

WOMAN   Yes, love. We can stay here for as long as you want.

He heaves his shoulders and releases a quivering breath.

MAN   Cheese. I can smell cheese.

WOMAN   We have a nice piece, love. We've a nice bit of fresh cheddar in the fridge. I got a pound block.

It was on special.

MAN   Special.

WOMAN   Special, love. I'll make us a sandwich with a nice bit of Spanish onion later. And we'll see if there's anything on the TV.

She waits for a reply, then moves in closer to him and resumes her caressing with both hands and kissing his neck. He clenches the bottle of nail varnish.

MAN   The black fur.

WOMAN   Yes, love. The rabbit fur, you mean? On the li'l hat I wore when I was expecting? Go on.

She removes her hand from his knuckles and moves it over his backside. She chuckles.

MAN   The animal fur.

WOMAN   Yes, Mursheen. It was rabbit.

He slumps and releases a loud breath.

What's the animal fur, love?

He stiffens.

MAN   It stays on the ground.

WOMAN   Does it, love?

MAN   It stays on the grass when the animal sinks into the ground.

WOMAN   Does it, love?

He goes rigid and his fists clench more tightly.

All the while the boy is doing his tricks on the

bicycle.

MAN   It stays on the grass.

WOMAN   Does it, love? Come on. Tell me all about it
        upstairs.

*He slumps. His head drops heavily. She whispers
very soothingly, and hooks an arm around his.*

Come on.

*Something alarms him and he lifts his head, as if
suddenly remembering. He becomes rigid. She
caresses him.*

Alright love. We can go up when you're ready.
No rush.

*She goes up on her toes and kisses his neck. This
goes on for a few moments. He raises a hand and
it reaches the cupboard door before her hand
catches up. This time it opens a fraction. She
guides his hand back down to the countertop. In
the other hand he begins rotating and thumbing
the nail varnish bottle.*

*The boy drops the bicycle to the floor with a
clatter, paces around in boredom for a few
moments. He has earphones in his pocket that he
puts in his ears. A tune enters his head and he
begins to dance some hip-hop moves, slowly and
clumsily at first but then he gets into a rhythm.*

I got a nice piece of ray for dinner.

MAN   Ray.

WOMAN   It was on special. I was lucky.

She chuckles and rubs his knuckles and back and kisses the his neck. She quickly touches her hair then returns her hand to his knuckles.

MAN   Lucky.

WOMAN   It was the last piece they had. Vinnie said he'd put it on special for me.

She chuckles again, and waits for a response. His body sways slightly and his head moves as if preparing to say something distressing but can't get it out.

Don't worry, love. I'll do it in the microwave (*she leans in to kiss him*). That way there won't be any smell (*she kisses him again*).

He raises a hand from the counter and tilts his head back, grabbing his forehead.

MAN   Fucking hell (*uttered nervously*).

She rubs him gently.

WOMAN   It's alright, love. It's alright.

He puts his hand back on the countertop.

MAN   America and Peru and Mexico...

WOMAN   Yes, love. All those places. Sure they've got their own problems to take care of too.

He shakes his head slowly and with control from side to side, breathing a long breath through his teeth.

The boy stops dancing and takes out the headphones, starts pacing again. He puts his hand on his head in mild exasperation.

What, love? What about America and what have you?

MAN The Indians were so wise.

WOMAN Ah, the Comanches and what have you. You can tell they're wise just by looking at their faces, can't you love? Even on the old black and white.

MAN The black and white.

She chuckles and briskly rubs his back and then pats it like she was burping a child.

WOMAN Remember the Bosch? We hardly know ourselves since we got the new Japanese color, do we Mursheen? We'd be lost without it.

He doesn't answer, just remains rigid and she waits, considering what next to say. The boy makes his first sound.

BOY I-I-I-I, I-I/I-I-I

This is repeated—no melody, an inane sound aimed at hearing his own voice.

MAN They close their eyes chewing their food.

WOMAN Do they, love?

MAN So fucking wise.

The boy sits on the ground beside the bicycle. Then he lies on his side, his front, his back, readjusting his position restlessly. He picks at things on the ground. He scowls, frowns, glances suddenly up and around him, as if after an insect flitting around.

WOMAN   You know, love, that reminds me…

She hesitates, stops to think.

I can't remember what I was going to say now.

She remembers.

Oh, that's right. The program about the Comanche Indians, where they had to live, and all the li'l ways they had for pitching their wigwams in the marshes. Remember love?

For the first time, he nods his head. The nodding is very slight, but the encouragement she reads from it is tremendous.

Yes, yes love, wasn't that an amazing program! And the, eh…what the…the squaws and their li'l pigtails carrying the water round their necks. Remember?

When she says the word 'neck' focus is drawn to her own conspicuous neck again.

The boy, on the ground, puts his hands behind his neck, stretches out, looks over and pays attention.

Remember, love?

He nods his head again slightly. It encourages her again.

Yes, it was an amazing program. They had it rough, didn't they love, the poor squaws. They'd scream, wouldn't they, if they…what was it again?

MAN   They can't be touched.

WOMAN   Ah, that's right. Not until they ask to be or
        something, wasn't it?

        *He nods slightly. She caresses him and remembers
        she hasn't kissed him for a while, so she leans over
        and kisses him on the neck.*

        We watched that program the last time,
        remember (*chuckles*)?....after we came back
        down.

        *Her voice becomes very soft as she strokes his
        back and hand.*

        And we had a nice bit of smoked cod from
        Vinnie. He gave it to me on special. It must have
        been a Friday as well.

        *He releases a quivering breath and his body
        appears to shake. She leans over to kiss him.*

        I steamed it on the pan, love, remember? So
        there wouldn't be any smell.

        *He stops shaking and his body goes quite limp.
        She hooks an arm around his.*

        Come on, love. Let's go.

        *She gets his hand off the countertop and pulls his
        arm, making his body come away slightly but his
        face remains unseen. She begins to feel resistance
        and a hint of imperiousness comes in her face.*

        Come on, Mursheen. Let's go upstairs.

        *He stiffens suddenly, as if coming out of a trance
        and puts his hand back down on the counter,*

returning to his position. She sniffs to clear her nose and touches her hair. While his left hand is unattended he makes a reach for the cupboard, but she intercepts him, and the door remains shut, both hands returning to the counter. She resumes her caressing all over again—she doesn't seem to know how to stop.

But now there is no kissing and there is a slight gap between caresses. His head is not hanging but raised and mobile.

The boy takes off his shoe and then slowly peels off his sock, sniffs it, puts it aside. Then he starts to pick his toes. As he does so he smells his fingers.

MAN   What about the one about cancer?

WOMAN   Was that on after?

MAN   *(nodding).* Cervical cancer.

WOMAN   I don't think I remember, love.

MAN   The causes and treatments.

WOMAN   Oh right.

MAN   The risk factors.

Pause.

It's how your mother went.

WOMAN   Must be awful for people all the same, mustn't it love?

He nods. He collects himself after the exertion. His head slumps a little. She goes on rubbing him. He reaches a hand up but stops himself before reaching the cupboard and before she reacts.

I can make us a nice drop of stew, if you'd like, instead.

He slumps more and releases a loud breath and shakes his head with great control again, as before, from side to side.

It won't take me a minute, love, to nip down to Vinnie...(*she leans over and kisses his neck*)...see if he has a nice bit of steak. I'll see if he'll mince a nice piece of sirloin for me.

She goes on kissing.

He might have it on special.

The boy has taken off the other shoe and sock and is picking the toes on his other foot.

MAN   Special.

WOMAN   You never know, love.

She puts a hand on his backside and holds it there, waiting. She sniffs and the sound sends a shock through him. He stiffens and raises his head.

MAN   What about the Dutch?

She starts rubbing his backside. He weakens slightly.

WOMAN   The program you mean, love? I don't remember that one. What was that one about?

MAN   Rotterdam.

WOMAN   Was it, love?

He shakes his head and slumps a little. Then reaches a hand up to the cupboard door. She lets him open it and slide a hand inside before she takes his arm by the wrist and pulls it out, back down. Then she raises her own hand again to shut the door.

What's Waterdam, love? Tell me.

MAN   Rotterdam. It's a large port.

She goes on rubbing patiently but says nothing. He moves his head, thinking of what to say next, and listening for her words.

The biggest port in Europe.

WOMAN   Must be something else, love, I'd imagine.

He seems struck by this remark.

MAN   Imagine.

WOMAN   Sure, wouldn't there be all sorts there, love, in a place like that?

MAN   Not all sorts.

WOMAN   Really, love? I'd have thought you'd see all sorts in a place like that.

He slumps and nods slightly. Then shakes his head with his usual control.

MAN   You don't see children.

Her caresses become more urgent. She leans over and kisses him on the neck.

WOMAN   That sounds like an awful place. No children.

He drops his head slightly, shifting his weight

between his feet.

MAN   All you see is prostitutes.

WOMAN   A place like that would give you the yucks, love, wouldn't it?

She shivers as if disgusted and rattles her cheeks.

By now the boy has put back on his trainers without his socks—his socks are left on the stage. He is picking his nose slowly and looking at the product, rolling it around in his finger and thumb.

She goes back to caressing him. Neither of them speaks for a moment.

The boy resumes his tuneless music, jerking his body erratically to the rhythm.

BOY   I-I-I-I, I-I/I-I-I

She starts to hum a tune of her own, also quite tuneless and self-conscious. As both of them make their noises the man raises his head and moves it restlessly, in some distress, as if his thinking were being deliberately sabotaged.

This goes on for quite a long time. It feels like she and the boy are digging in for the long haul. His frustration grows and manifests in slight movements of his body. He looks at the nail varnish bottle in his hand.

WOMAN   Ah!!!

She stops caressing and removes her hand from his knuckles to touch the arm on his back. The boy stops humming too and quickly pulls his pants down and hunkers to take a shit. The t-shirt covers his privates.

MAN   What?

WOMAN   Oh it's just this fecking tennis elbow.

He goes rigid.

It'll be gone in a minute, love, don't worry. The pain comes and goes.

MAN   Tennis.

WOMAN   It's from all the painting. I'm not used to the roller yet. The fecking weight of it.

He looks a little to the left and right at the messy paintwork on the walls, and considers it. She observes this and takes her time before going on.

It'll need a second coat I'd say.

He slumps deeply and releases a breath. His legs seem to buckle.

She resumes her caressing but it is awkward on account of her elbow pain. She soldiers on.

I'm nearly finished, love. It'll be grand when it's finished. It'll be worth it.

He shakes his head slowly. She is encouraged by this.

I might go and see Vinnie. Maybe I can get him to do us a favor. Let's see if it gets any worse first.

He shifts his weight and his shoulders heave.

If it gets any worse I can nip down and see

Vinnie.

He raises a hand to the cupboard. It stops halfway and his arm trembles quite violently. She watches it but does nothing. It starts to come back down but then he forces it back up to the cupboard. When it reaches the door she covers it with her own hand, and both hands return to the countertop.

We can usually rely on Vinnie, can't we Mursheen? For all his faults.

She leans over and kisses him on the neck. Meanwhile, the boy has finished taking a shit, turns to took at it and now starts to search for something to wipe himself with. He searches his pockets around his ankles. He takes out an ipod, keys, a condom, coins. No good. Then he looks around the floor. He sees his socks and shuffles over on his hunkers to get one. He wipes himself with it, examines it carefully, bringing it close to his face, then throws it far away to the front of the stage, towards the audience. He pulls up his jeans.

He's doing well for himself, Vinnie. He's done a grand job on his own house, so he has. He's painted the whole place. Real fresh colors.

She says 'fresh colors' like a child just after looking into a brown paper bag at the candy inside given to her by an unfamiliar adult.

It reminds me of Jacob's. They'd a lovely fresh

coat of paint on the walls. It used to put us all in good form in the mornings.

He looks up at the walls again, the partial coating of fresh paint, a lemon color. He turns slightly, thinking of something hopeful, as if for the first time.

MAN   Jacob's.

WOMAN   The biscuit factory, love, where I used to work.

His hope deflates and he slumps again against the countertop. His legs buckle and she uses her hands to support him, get him back up again onto his feet. He goes back to his original pose and she resumes her stroking. The boy is pushing the bicycle around the floor with his foot. His head is hanging. It is as if he has forgotten he could do tricks on it.

For a while nobody speaks. The woman is patient, and mechanical.

In time the man's head lifts a little and starts to move, indicating an urge to speak again.

MAN   Was I brave, you think?

WOMAN   Yes (*unusually brief*).

MAN   Was I really brave?

WOMAN   Yes, love. You were.

MAN   Was it really bravery?

WOMAN   I think so, love.

He is perturbed by the doubt implied.

MAN   I don't remember.

WOMAN   You were very brave.

MAN   Am I brave, do you think?

WOMAN   Yes, love.

MAN   Am I brave enough?

WOMAN   I think so. You were brave enough before.

MAN   I can be brave.

WOMAN   I know you can, love.

MAN   You know?

WOMAN   I think so.

MAN   If I hide my fear.

WOMAN   There's nothing to be afraid of.

She leans over and kisses his neck, running her tongue along it and stroking his backside with her hand at the same time. It is a carefully coordinated act. His body stiffens, his buttocks contract.

Later, we'll have a nice bit of dinner and see what's on the TV.

He nods his head slightly, as if beginning to surrender. She rubs his back.

And I'll give you a good mind.

His body relaxes and he releases a long breath.

All you need is a good mind, Mursheen. That's all. You just need to be minded.

She leans over again and extends her tongue as

far as it will go to reach into his ear. She flickers it against his earlobe, and at the same time runs her hand again over his backside. He shudders, quivers. She chuckles.

Come on, Mursheen.

She takes his arm and tries to lead him off again. But he holds tight. She stands still a moment, a bit impatiently, and waits, holding out her arm.

MAN   Why don't I remember?

WOMAN   You do remember, love.

MAN   How do you know?

WOMAN   You remember everything.

MAN   I don't remember being brave.

WOMAN   That's just because you're in a different mood now.

MAN   What kind of mood was I in before?

WOMAN   A different mood, love.

The boy starts stomping on the wheels of the bicycle.

You were more open.

MAN   Open.

WOMAN   Remember?

MAN   I remember I was always in this mood.

WOMAN   No, love.

MAN   You can't be sure.

WOMAN   Yes, love. I'm sure.

MAN   Are you really sure?

WOMAN   Yes, love. I'm sure.

MAN   How can you be sure?

WOMAN   I'm just sure.

She resumes her caressing.

MAN   But how?

She takes her time to answer, first leaning over to kiss his raised, exasperated neck.

WOMAN   My nail varnish.

She chuckles. He looks down suddenly at the bottle clenched in his fist, that he's been thumbing and rotating.

MAN   This?

WOMAN   Uh-huh.

She leans in and flickers her tongue at his ear as he concentrates on the nail varnish bottle.

You were more horny before (*she whispers these words*).

He quivers and his legs buckle.

You touched your hard cock...(*drops voice to a whisper*)... it felt like an orgy.

MAN   (*wobbling, then correcting his balance*). An orgy is a group of people.

She leans in to kiss him.

WOMAN   That's right, love.

MAN   Then how was it like an orgy if it was just me?

WOMAN	Yes, love.
MAN	No, I'm asking how could it have been like an orgy.
WOMAN	It just felt like it, love.
MAN	But that isn't an orgy.
WOMAN	Yes, love.
MAN	Do you not understand what an orgy is?
WOMAN	You tell me, love.
MAN	It's a group of swingers having sex.
WOMAN	Is it, love?
MAN	Yes. And do you even know what swingers are?
WOMAN	Yes, love.
MAN	Do you?
WOMAN	No, love. Tell me.
MAN	Swingers are people who engage in casual sex.
WOMAN	Are they, love?
MAN	Yes.
WOMAN	Oh right.
MAN	So you couldn't have felt like an orgy around me.
WOMAN	Yes, love.

They are both silent for a while. He seems calmer, a little encouraged by the contention. He seems to have reclaimed some ground.

The boy has taken a can of paint from his pocket and begun to spray graffiti—words and diagrams—on the wall. ORGY, COCK, a symbol of copulation, SEX, a cock and balls, a figure masturbating.

MAN   Bravery always comes at a price.

WOMAN   Does it, love?

He nods his head, a bit more assertively than before.

Why is that?

MAN   You finally have to pay the piper.

WOMAN   Do you, love?

He nods.

Why do you have to pay for the paper?

MAN   The piper. Pay the piper.

WOMAN   Oh, the piper.

She chuckles.

MAN   Because you can't be brave all the time.

WOMAN   Everyone has good and bad days, love.

MAN   If you slip up just once, you might as well never have been brave.

WOMAN   How come, love?

MAN   You have to pay back for all those times you were brave for nothing.

She leans over and kisses him on the neck.

WOMAN   You'll always be brave, love.

He slumps and releases a heavy breath.

MAN   And if I'm not?

WOMAN   You will be.

MAN   Are you sure?

WOMAN   I think so, love.

She rubs his backside and tongues his ear. They are quiet for a long time.

He raises his head and listens for her to speak or give him some sort of cue.

She has turned her face away, and is staring off into space in a daydream. An ambiguous smile crosses her face.

The caressing of his back and knuckles becomes purely mechanical, all concentration she had been putting into it now going into other thoughts which have either nothing to do with him, or at least nothing to do with seducing him. Here she is at her most detached.

He grows nervous, appears ridiculous, as if being persecuted by a weakling he could defeat if only he had the initiative to fight back.

He lifts the left hand off the counter, from under her caress, and brings it up to rub his neck where she has been kissing. Then he puts it back on the countertop.

He looks at the bottle of nail varnish in his other hand, and then sets it back down on the countertop.

They both hold their position without speaking. Finally he releases a noise like a bark.

MAN   Yah!

He coughs to clear his throat. Her only reaction is to return her hand to cover his left knuckles again. He releases a breath forcibly but patiently.

The boy runs out of paint. He shakes the can and puts it to his ear. Then he throws it away, towards the audience, as for the shit-stained sock. He paces the floor and begins shadow boxing.

I was thinking about the place in the country.

WOMAN   What place?

MAN   The place in the country.

WOMAN   Whitehead, you mean?

MAN   This time of year I do think about the mulberry tree there.

WOMAN   They're like sloes or something, you said.

MAN   A bit like sloes. Now would be the time to prune.

WOMAN   Would it?

MAN   It would.

She lets out a little puff of air. Then she sniffs. She doesn't speak. Her rubbing becomes erratic, careless.

WOMAN   You have to have something to look forward to don't you?

He nods.

But there isn't a hope of you going to Whitehead.

MAN There is.

WOMAN How is there?

MAN There has to be.

WOMAN Then go.

MAN You can't just go.

WOMAN You see what I mean.

MAN You can't just up and go like that.

WOMAN That's what I mean.

MAN It's for looking forward to.

WOMAN But when will you actually go?

MAN It's for looking forward to. It's not for going to.

She releases another puff of air and sniffs. Then she smiles ambiguously again.

You've got to have something at the back of your mind all the time.

WOMAN I don't see the point when you can go there just as easily.

MAN There is a point.

WOMAN Well...

MAN There is a point.

WOMAN If you say so, love.

MAN No. The point is if you went you'd have to find something else to look forward to. Something better.

She sniffs.

And nothing I could imagine is better than

Whitehead.

WOMAN   It's only a scrap of waste ground in the middle of nowhere.

MAN   That doesn't matter.

WOMAN   That doesn't matter?

She takes her hands off him completely and clenches her fists by her side.

MAN   It doesn't matter.

WOMAN   Then what does matter?

He shifts his weight and drops his head, a touch shamefully.

MAN   That it's better than this.

She looks like she is about to explode, her chin juts and her head tilts to show this. But suddenly she controls herself and chuckles ironically instead.

WOMAN   But it's unlivable up there! Sure there isn't even a septic tank. There's only a soakaway.

She chuckles again.

He twitches his head to think about a response, but he fails and finally drops his head and releases a heavy breath. She puts her hand up under his sweater once again and the other hand on his knuckles.

We could probably get Vinnie to go up and take a look at it.

He seems to buckle but stays standing, his arms

tremble. She seems not to notice, or to ignore it.

He put the septic tank in, in his own house himself.

He shakes his head very slightly, under tight control.

He got rid of the old soakaway. The smell used to be awful whenever it rained he told me.

He tries to nod and recover.

He and Mary don't know themselves anymore with the septic tank.

After a flurry of punches the boy leans on his knees to rest.

The man nods. She leans over and kisses him.

Come one, love. Let's go. You smell so masculine.

He doesn't move. She wraps her arms around his arm and tries to draw him away.

Come on, Mursheen Durkin.

He doesn't move.

Come on. We'll have a nice bit of ray in the microwave when we come back down. Come on.

His arm comes loose from the counter and his body begins to turn. We see the edge of his face, and are about to see it all it seems. We are afraid of what his face will look like.

Come on. There might be something good on the TV after.

Come on, the hoovering can wait till tomorrow.

He resists, and forces his hand back onto the counter. She lets it go with undisguised irritation but in a flash returns to her ambiguous smile.

For a moment she stands by watching him without any touching.

He raises a trembling hand up towards the cupboard. It stops halfway, for a moment. She watches it and folds her arms.

He raises his hand the rest of the way and stops at the handle. She watches it, puts her hands down by her sides again. His hand remains there, unmoving and uninterrupted for a long time. She folds her arms again.

The boy goes to the front of the stage, puts his hands in his pockets and looks out blankly at the audience. He makes barely perceptible and intermittent dance moves that he seems to forget or lose interest in every few seconds.

Open it, go on.

She waits. He doesn't move.

Go on.

The boy turns his back to the audience. He stands still a moment, and then slowly paces out the distance to the back of the stage. As he passes the bicycle he kicks it though it's not in the way. At the back of the stage he turns and stands against the wall facing the audience with his hands by his side, feet together, staring straight ahead.

I dare you.

The boy reaches into his pocket for a blindfold but there is nothing there. He pulls the baseball cap peak down over his eyes.

The man opens the door wide enough for his hand and inserts it. We don't see what's inside. The hand remains like that for a while. He agonizes there. She watches.

The boy waits.

All is silent for quite a while. Only the sound of bottles and glasses clinking inside the cupboard.

It's your choice.

The boy pulls the baseball cap down further over his face.

The clinking of glasses stops. The man seems to be thinking.

Think about it.

Silence and still. She juts a foot out and folds her arms.

Think how much of the claim is left.

MAN   The claim.

WOMAN   It won't last forever. Do you even have any idea how much is left?

He stops clinking and moving his hand.

"The little man who knows it all." Isn't that what your mother would have called you? "The little man who knows it all."

She chuckles. He clinks the bottles and glasses.

"The little man who never stops thinking. There's a smell of burning—it's only the little man's brain at work, not to worry."

He stops moving his hand.

Go on. I dare you. If you know how much of the claim is left.

He holds his position for a while. She says nothing and does not move.

The boy holds his position too.

She sniffs. He starts clinking the bottles and the glasses in the cupboard again.

Slowly she starts to break down, her body begins to sag slightly. He senses this.

The boy puts his hand in his back pocket and takes out a gat made from a coat hanger, elastic bands and piece of plastic. He finds small objects on the floor near where he is standing. He picks them up and fires them out into the audience.

She speaks with a cracking voice, full of sarcasm.

"It's all under strict control. Not to worry."

He too begins to show new signs of distress. She speaks on.

"Don't take any notice. It's perfectly normal."

She chuckles but because she's also crying the sarcasm is clearer.

"It'll be over soon. Then we can all relax again."

She sniffs.

"Not to worry. It'll be grand."

The boy suddenly gets away from the wall, zig-zags across the floor, kneels and fires more ammo from his gat. Cover, crawl, observe, fire.

"The trick is to get something out there."

She chuckles with bitter irony.

"It doesn't matter what it is. It doesn't matter how. Just get something out there. Then it'll be grand."

She cries a bit harder now, and cannot speak. He drops his hand down from the cupboard. The door closes shut again. He puts his knuckles back on the countertop.

MAN   "Later you can make sense of it. When it's just a memory."

She cries harder.

He extends the hand that has been reaching up to the cupboard behind him. It remains extended as she cries and keeps her own hands to herself.

He opens and closes his hand to signal for her to take it. She hesitates before releasing a mighty sob, and then timidly placing her hand in his as if it were a painful act of surrender. She is very reluctant but falling apart and without resistance.

The boy, having darted here and there and fired off all his ammo, picks up his bicycle and leaves the stage.

He pulls her arm into his, around his belly and draws her closer. She allows herself to be pulled reluctantly.

When he gets her in closer—she is shaking now and crying, her head dipped forward—he stands up straight for the first time. He puts his other hand back and takes her other hand, pulls it around to complete the embrace and holds them in position. She buries her face in his back, between his shoulder blades and begins convulsing. His head is raised up to the ceiling/cupboard, his body composed.

We have never seen his face fully, and now her face is no longer visible.

Curtain

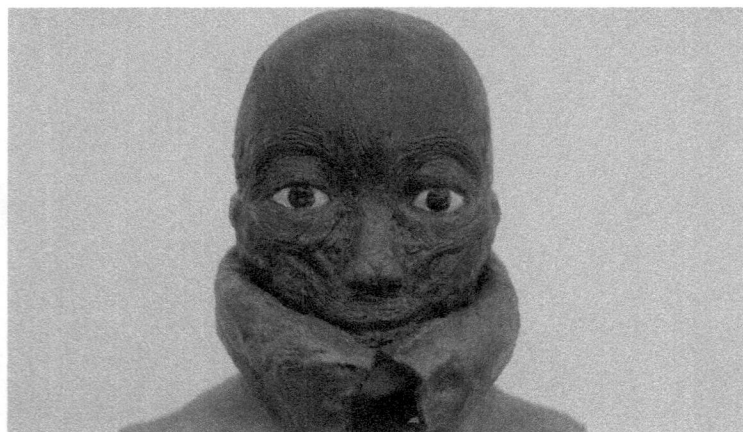

HOLD STILL

CHARACTERS

Man

Woman

Teenaged boy

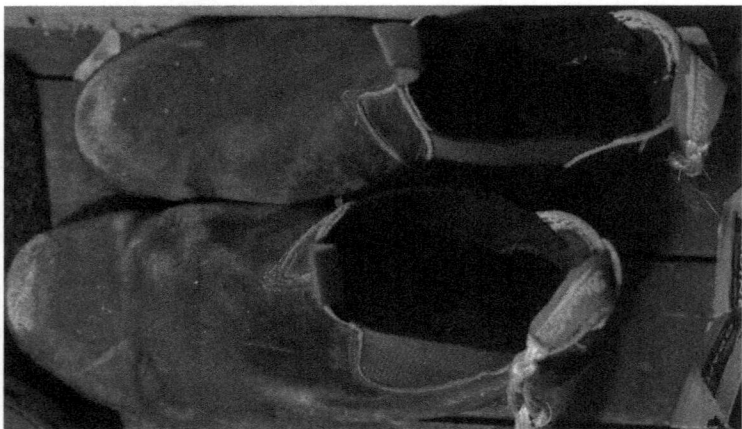

PALLIATIVE CARE

Protect me from my father
protect me from my mother
protect me from my brother
protect me from my sister
protect me from my son
protect me from my daughter
protect me from other men
protect me from other women
protect me and love me
      —whoever you are.

Scene: Man and woman in the kitchen of their house. He is sitting on a chair placed in the middle of the floor with his back to the audience, his upper body shrouded in a nylon cape. She is standing over him, cutting his hair. We see the nape of his neck, which she works on carefully while circling him, cutting and talking.

He is soothed, almost hypnotized by her incidental touches during the clipping. He seems like a boy, sitting on a low chair, having his hair cropped close to his head.

She combs his hair very slowly. The scissors makes a loud and pleasant rasp with each cut. She sprays his head with a mist of water from time to time to keep it damp. She occasionally blows on his neck to brush away the hairs.

MAN   This is how the rot starts.

WOMAN   Mmm.

MAN   Did you know that?

WOMAN   Mmm.

MAN   How do you know?

WOMAN   Hold still.

MAN   How do you know?

WOMAN   What?

MAN   How do you know?

WOMAN   How do I know what?

MAN   How do you know about the rot starting?

WOMAN   What rot?

MAN   Yeah. What rot?

Silence.

You're not paying attention to me.

WOMAN   What?

MAN   You don't listen to what I have to say.

WOMAN   *(laughs).* Would you feck off. Hold still or I'll stab you.

MAN   Go on, then. Stab me.

WOMAN   What are you talking about?

She holds the scissors and comb aloft in her outspread arms.

MAN   You might as well get it over with. Maybe then you'll listen to what I have to say.

WOMAN   I'm listening to you.

MAN   Well you're not hearing.

WOMAN   What are you talking about?

MAN   Make a clean breast of it at least.

WOMAN   You're mad. You're talking gibberish.

MAN   Yeah, gibberish.

WOMAN   Gibberish, bejaysus.

MAN   Yeah.

WOMAN   No wonder people don't be able to follow you half the time.

MAN   What people?

WOMAN   Never mind.

MAN   No, what people?

WOMAN   Nobody. Hold still.

MAN   Who are you talking about?

WOMAN   It doesn't matter.

MAN   Of course it matters. Who?

WOMAN   Oh, you think it's just you against the rest of the world, don't you?

MAN   What? What does that mean?

WOMAN   Poor you all alone having to face everyone else each day.

MAN   What are you talking about?

WOMAN   Yeah. What am I talking about.

MAN   What?

WOMAN   Do I have to paint you a picture?

MAN   Who are these people?

WOMAN   You know who they are.

MAN   Tell me.

WOMAN   You know who they are.

MAN   Who are they?

WOMAN   Hold still.

MAN   Who are they, I'm asking you?

WOMAN   *(laughs).* Hold still!

MAN   Who?

WOMAN   Gerry and so forth.

MAN	Gerry? His feet stink.
WOMAN	*(laughs).* What?
MAN	His feet stink to high heavens.
WOMAN	I wouldn't have thought that now.
MAN	You can smell them from the next room.
WOMAN	Gerry always struck me as a neat chap.
MAN	What's neatness got to do with it?
WOMAN	Have it your way, but he always appeared neat to me. I always said he had lovely teeth.
MAN	I'm saying what's being neat got to do with having rotten feet.
WOMAN	Alright.
MAN	No, you're doing it again. How would being neat mean he didn't have smelly feet?
WOMAN	I'm just saying.
MAN	No. You're not. Couldn't he have just played a football match and then put on a suit and new shoes without washing himself first?
WOMAN	Whatever you say. Hold still.
MAN	No, I'm asking you. Couldn't he?
WOMAN	Gerry's a good boy.
MAN	Sure how would you notice if his feet were stinking in any case?
WOMAN	Yeah.
MAN	Your own feet stink like a bejaysus soldier's.
WOMAN	Do they.

MAN	It's disgusting. And to make it worse you don't even realize it, do you?
WOMAN	I guess not.
MAN	No, you guess not. I do have to fumigate the room when you leave in the morning.
WOMAN	Do you.
MAN	It takes an hour to clear.
WOMAN	Does it?
MAN	And pick up your dirty underwear and put them in the wash basket.
WOMAN	Oh right.
MAN	Yes right. Shit stained and everything they do be when I find them in the corner of the bedroom.
WOMAN	*(laughs).* Hold still.
MAN	Do you not have any shame?
WOMAN	What?
MAN	Have you no sense of shame?
WOMAN	*(laughs).* I suppose I mustn't.
MAN	I suppose so too.
WOMAN	Mmm.
MAN	You couldn't have, sure.
WOMAN	No.
MAN	No. That wouldn't make any sense, the way you lead your life.
WOMAN	Yeah.

MAN   Yeah. It's not your fault of course.

WOMAN   No.

MAN   No. It's just who you are.

WOMAN   Mmm.

MAN   Yeah. You can't change who you are.

WOMAN   Hold still.

MAN   You must realize that, though.

WOMAN   Mmm.

MAN   Don't you?

WOMAN   What?

MAN   Realize that.

WOMAN   Realize what?

MAN   That you can't change who you are.

WOMAN   *(laughs).* Why would I change who I am?

MAN   I would.

WOMAN   Would you?

MAN   Yeah.

WOMAN   I see.

MAN   Do you?

WOMAN   Mmm.

MAN   I'd change in a flash.

WOMAN   Who would you be?

                   Laughs and mockingly rolls her eyes.

MAN   Who would I be?

WOMAN   Somebody nice?

MAN   No. I wouldn't be anybody. If I were YOU I'd change, is what I'm saying.

WOMAN   Oh.

MAN   You don't hear a word I say, do you?

WOMAN   I hear most of it.

MAN   You hear what you want to hear.

WOMAN   I suppose so.

MAN   I suppose so.

WOMAN   Hold still.

MAN   Are you nearly finished?

WOMAN   Almost. You've a few bits still sticking up.

MAN   Well just cut them off and be done with it.

WOMAN   I'm trying. You can't just cut them off like that.

MAN   Why not?

WOMAN   You'll have a hole in your head.

MAN   A bare patch you mean?

WOMAN   More than one.

MAN   I don't care at this stage.

WOMAN   *(laughs).* You'll look even madder than usual.

Silence for a while.

Hold still.

Silence.

I'll have to see Dr. Whiting about more sick certs this week.

Silence.

We're almost out.

Silence.

I'll see if he can let me have them again without you having to see him.

Silence.

Anyway, let's see. He did me a favor the last time.

Silence.

(She laughs a lucky laugh.) How we'd survive without those sick certs God only knows.

Silence.

Thank God for that little job I have with Dr. Whiting.

Silence.

Even if the pay is not worth talking about.

Silence.

We'd be lost without it.

Silence.

Sure how else would we get the sick certs?

Silence.

Hold still.

MAN   What makes his teeth so special?

WOMAN   What?

MAN   What's so special about his teeth?

WOMAN	Dr. Whiting's?
MAN	His as well?
WOMAN	Whose teeth?
MAN	Gerry's teeth.
WOMAN	What?
MAN	You think everyone has lovely teeth.
WOMAN	But his are nice and white.
MAN	It's because you haven't any teeth of our own.

Silence.

You haven't a tooth left in your head.

Silence.

I do have to watch you shoving those dentures back into your mouth every morning.

Silence.

At least it's dark when you take them out.

WOMAN	Hold still.
MAN	It's not your fault I know. It's just bad genes. Your whole family's toothless. Not a natural tooth between the lot of them.
WOMAN	Brandon had his own teeth.
MAN	Brandon doesn't count. He died before the rot had a chance to set in.

Silence.

Now, I've nothing against Brandon, I liked him as a person. He was like a younger brother to me. I'm just saying he would have been toothless like the rest of you had he lived.

Silence.

Do you not agree with me?

Silence.

Do you not agree with me?

WOMAN Hold still.

MAN Why can't you admit the truth?

WOMAN The truth about what?

MAN About Brandon's teeth. Toothless wonders the lot of you. Mouths like a sewer.

Silence.

Well?

WOMAN Well what?

MAN What do you have to say about it?

Silence.

Well?

WOMAN Whatever you like.

MAN So you're admitting I'm right then.

WOMAN If you say so.

MAN Well that's all you had to say. It's not like you're surrendering to an enemy. It's only conversation.

WOMAN Mmm.

MAN I know I'm right. I got a book from the library about genetics.

WOMAN   Mmm.

MAN   It tells you all about the different genes and chromosomes you inherit from your mother and your father after they have sexual intercourse. When they fuck each other in other words.

WOMAN   Mmm.

MAN   It's a fascinating book. I'll let you look at it later. You can read it yourself if you want. It's not due back until Thursday.

WOMAN   Mmm.

MAN   Or do you want me to call up the librarian and ask them to extend if for another week.

WOMAN   No.

MAN   You'd probably need a fortnight, or longer, the way you read, in snatches.

        Silence.

        You don't like factual books, do you?

WOMAN   Not really. Hold still.

MAN   You prefer romances. "Escapist literature". You don't like books that explain the mysteries of life, genetics, sexual reproduction, libido...do you even know what libido is? What the word libido means?

WOMAN   What?

MAN   Libido.

WOMAN   Libido?

MAN   Yeah. Libido.

WOMAN   No, tell me.

MAN   Well, do you want to know?

WOMAN   Something to do with genetics.

MAN   But do you know what?

WOMAN   No.

MAN   Will I tell you?

            Silence.

            What? Will I tell you in plain terms?

WOMAN   Go on.

MAN   It means horniness. Your horniness is your
            libido.

WOMAN   Oh.

MAN   You didn't know that now, did you?

WOMAN   No.

MAN   Your horniness, your desire to fuck. It's
            explained in the book. Published in Cambridge.

            Silence.

            I'm telling you it's in the book I got from the
            library. But I'm wasting my breath. You won't
            read it, will you?

            Silence.

            Will you?

WOMAN   Will I what?

MAN   Bother to read the book.

WOMAN	For what?
MAN	You see what I mean?
WOMAN	Yeah.
MAN	What?
WOMAN	Hold still
MAN	What do you mean "yeah"? Do you see what I mean?
WOMAN	About what? Hold still.
MAN	About reading the book on genetics.
WOMAN	Sure why would I need to read it when I've got you to explain it all to me (*laughs*)?
MAN	Yeah. Sure.
WOMAN	(*sighs*).

Silence.

Just in case, would you be able to come to Dr. Whiting's surgery on Thursday morning?

Silence.

It's usually quiet before 11.

Silence.

He might see you quick. Then I can issue the sick certs for the next few weeks.

Silence.

I'm sure I can get him to see you quick, in between the scheduled patients. He mightn't charge us anything.

Silence.

Anyway, we'll see.

Silence.

You'll be nice and presentable with your new haircut.

Silence.

A bit more off the top and it'll be finished, then you can go and shake the hairs off out in the back.

Silence.

MAN	Did you not hear a word I said?
WOMAN	What?
MAN	Did you listen to a single word I said?
WOMAN	I listened to it all, about genetics.
MAN	Genetics. Genetics. GENETICS!
WOMAN	Genetics. Isn't that how you pronounce it?
MAN	No.
WOMAN	Isn't it? It sounded like genetics to me, whatever it is.
MAN	Thursday!
WOMAN	What about Thursday? I only asked if you're free on Thursday morning.
MAN	And didn't I tell you before that I had to return the book on genetics to the library on Thursday?
WOMAN	Oh right. That's all you had to say.
MAN	I did say it! But you didn't hear me. And then I

said AFTER that, do you want to read the book.

WOMAN   I heard you.

MAN   But you didn't answer me. I offered to call the librarian up for you, and see if they would give you an extension for another week or a fortnight. Save me a trip up to the library.

WOMAN   I heard you.

MAN   But you didn't answer!

WOMAN   But the library is open all day.

MAN   What's that got to do with it?

WOMAN   Dr. Whiting only needs to see you in the morning.

MAN   Yeah. And?

WOMAN   Well, I thought you could drop your book off any time after that.

MAN   Any time after that? Do you know anything about me at all?

WOMAN   Oh for God's sake.

MAN   Do you?

WOMAN   Yes, of course.

MAN   Then you know I always go to the library in the morning, when it's quiet, when I can think. When there's no fucking kids, or junkies, or teenagers, or whores clicking their heels up and down the steps outside.

Silence.

Do you know what it says on the wall outside

the library? Do you?

WOMAN   No.

MAN   No. How would you? You never go there. I'll tell you. It says "No Loitering". Do you know what loitering means?

WOMAN   No.

MAN   No. It means hanging around. Well who around here do you think understands what that sign means except for me? And why don't they hang the sign INSIDE the library as well as outside? Do you understand what I'm saying?

WOMAN   *(nods).*

MAN   Then maybe you can begin to understand some of the absurdities I have to contend with.

    Silence.

WOMAN   Hold still. I'm nearly finished.

    Silence.

    I'll see if Dr. Whiting will do me another favor then.

    Silence.

    He'll understand.

    Silence.

    He's used to seeing all sorts in that surgery.

    Silence.

    I don't know how he manages half the time.

Silence.

Hold still.

Longer silence.

After that last attack I thought he'd pack in the practice altogether.

Silence.

Little feckers.

Silence.

Sure he knew well who they were from their voices. They're all from around the corner, in Berryfield.

Silence.

They're patients with the surgery.

Silence.

He had to get the door fixed where they swung the whatchamacallit, the hatchet or whatever they had at it.

Silence.

He had to get bars put on the windows as well, all out of his own pocket. He said the Eastern Health Board doesn't cover that kind of thing.

Silence.

But sure they do just walk in, don't they, nowadays. During surgery hours. They don't give a feck, so they don't. What good will bars on the windows do? A waste of money.

Silence.

They pulled all the samples off the shelves, looking for the painkillers. Made a right haimes of the surgery. They left if in a shocking state.

Silence.

My heart does go out to Dr. Whiting

Silence.

Hold Still.

MAN	Why would they hit the door with the hatchet?
WOMAN	What?
MAN	You said they attack when he's open, didn't you?
WOMAN	During surgery hours.
MAN	That means when you're open, doesn't it? Or am I wrong?
WOMAN	I suppose so.
MAN	You suppose so? If they attack during surgery hours then why would they swing the hatchet at the door?
WOMAN	I don't know.
MAN	It doesn't make any sense, does it?
WOMAN	Mmm.
MAN	If the door was open there'd be no need to use the hatchet on it, would there?
WOMAN	No.

MAN   Then how do you explain what you just said?

WOMAN   I don't know.

MAN   Why would you strike a door if it was open?

WOMAN   I don't know.

MAN   But it doesn't make any sense.

WOMAN   They were wearing hoods when they came flying in. They probably wanted to scare us.

MAN   Flying in? Were they wearing wings as well?

WOMAN   Oh you know what I mean.

MAN   No, I don't. Say what you mean.

WOMAN   What?

MAN   You know what I'm like about accuracy. Or have you forgotten that as well?

WOMAN   Alright, when they stormed in.

MAN   But why did they strike at the door with the axe I'm asking.

WOMAN   I don't know. They just did!

MAN   But do you not see my point? That it makes no sense?

           Silence.

           No?

WOMAN   Yes.

           Silence.

MAN   I wish your heart would go out to me sometimes.

WOMAN   Hold still.

MAN   What's so special about Dr. Whiting?

Silence.

He'd keep a shotgun under the desk if he was any use. Disembowel the first one who came through the door in a mask.

Silence.

That's the only language they understand in Berryfield. I'd show them pain. Pain all the painkillers in the country wouldn't take away. I'd put them in their proper place. Bars on the windows. Fixing doors. What would he know about putting a bar on a window or fixing a door?

WOMAN   He's a doctor. He hires somebody for that type of thing.

MAN   What do you mean "that type of thing"? Real work you mean. As opposed to patting the chests of children and looking up old people's arses? And writing sick certs for men who can't find work?

Silence.

Sure why wouldn't your heart go out to him?

Silence.

What about me, (*thumbs his chest*) hah? Why doesn't your heart go out to me?

Silence.

To me, your husband. And not some culchie doctor with a lisp and long, wanker's fingers.

Silence.

What about me?

Longer silence.

WOMAN   *(laughs).* Oh poor Mursheen Durkin is feeling sorry for himself.

Silence.

Oh poor Mursheen Durkin is not getting enough attention. He feels neglected. Oh dear.

As she is talking she happens to prod him in the ear with the scissors.

MAN   You stupid cunt!

He puts his hand up to his ear and detects some blood.

Look what you've fucking done, you clumsy cunt!

He raises a foot and lashes out at her groin viciously, sending her flying backwards.

It's bad enough I have to sit here smelling your stinking breath and your stinking feet, and putting up with your stupidity without you stabbing me in the fucking ear as well. I could have lost my sense of hearing!

He stands up, pulls off the cape and throws it on the ground. It seems as if he will turn his face to the audience for the first time. But he doesn't.

Fuck it. Fuck the lot of you. I'm going out before I'm driven fucking crazy. Don't be here when I get back.

She gets up from the floor and starts to clean up the mess, holding her stomach. After a while the boy enters.

BOY   What's for dinner?

The woman looks at him with contempt, and studies him very carefully. She searches his face with deep bitterness and regret. Her emotions pass through a range but she does not speak. It's as if she doesn't recognize him, doesn't want to recognize him.

What's for dinner, Mam?

She pushes him out of her way and throws down the cape. He watches her for a while, cleaning up the mess while holding her stomach. She stops, sits down on the chair and quietly cries. He goes over to her and puts a hand on her shoulder.

Mam?

She ignores him and goes on crying. He stands there awkwardly. He removes his hand from her shoulder and waits.

Curtain

THE AUTHOR

George Saitoh is the penname of Gary Quinn. He was born in Dublin. He obtained a PhD in molecular biology from the University of York in 1999. He has worked at and published numerous scientific papers for private and public research organizations around the world including Syntex Chemicals Inc. (Boulder CO, USA), Institut Gustave Roussy (Paris), National Cancer Center Research Institute (Tokyo) and Novartis (Cambridge UK & Boston MA, USA). He currently lives in Tokyo where he teaches at Waseda University.

His art essays, translations, fiction and poetry have been published in *Kyoto Journal, Aeqai, Clarion, Word Riot* and *Orbis*. His plays have been staged in Tokyo and Dublin.

www.januscreations.com

www.georgesaitoh.com